Unleashing Your
Level 10 Life

Unleashing Your Level 10 Life

James Theros

Unleashing Your Level 10 Life.
Copyright © 2025 by James Theros. All rights reserved.

Printed in the United States of America. No part of this book may be used or reproduced in any manner whatsoever without written permission from the author. For information address:

Level 10 Publishing
854 Centerwood Dr.,
Tarpon Springs, FL 34688

Copies of this book may be purchased for educational, business, or sales promotional use. For information please write or email: Level 10 Publishing, 854 Centerwood Dr., Tarpon Springs, FL 34688 MasterTheros@yahoo.com

FIRST EDITION

ISBN: 978-0-9904164-3-2

Library of Congress Cataloging-in-Publication Data
Unleashing Your Level 10 Life, first edition, James Theros

Table of Contents

Preface vii

What Others Are Saying About Level 10 Martial Arts ix

1: The Silent Enemy, Mediocrity 1

2: Fall Down 7 Times, Get Up 8 7

3: The Power of Role Models 13

4: Discipline Over Excuses 19

5: Building Something from Nothing 25

6: Investing in Yourself 31

7: The Teacher Within 37

8: Respect, Focus, Discipline 43

9: The Level 10 Leader 49

10: Overcoming Family Struggles 55

11: The Fight for Excellence 61

12: Living at Level 10 67

Epilogue: Your Next Level 73

Preface

When I was seven years old, I walked into an after-school martial arts program not knowing that I was about to find my life's calling. The mats were worn, the movements foreign, and the discipline strict, but I felt alive in a way I had never felt before. I knew right then that martial arts would shape the rest of my life.

That journey, however, has been anything but smooth. I've stumbled, been distracted, made mistakes, and even spent years stuck at the same belt rank because I didn't stay consistent. I've struggled as a business owner, nearly lost my school because I didn't know what I was doing, and endured difficult family circumstances that could have easily defined me in bitterness instead of growth.

But through every setback, one thing remained: the belief that mediocrity was not an option. The world doesn't need more people settling for "good enough." It needs parents who will model excellence for their kids. Teachers who will demand the best from their students. Leaders who will guide with both strength and humility. And individuals, students of life, who will decide that "average" is not their destiny.

Over the decades, I've discovered that living a **Level 10 Life** is about much more than martial arts. Yes, the training gave me the tools, discipline, focus, respect, but the lessons apply everywhere. They apply when you're raising children in a world that doesn't always share your values. They apply when you're leading a team of employees who look to you for direction. They apply when you're a student learning to fight against distraction and doubt.

This book is not about me, it's about you. It's about unlocking the power that's already inside you, and unleashing it in a way that inspires others. You don't have to be a martial artist to live at Level

10. You just have to be willing to trade mediocrity for mastery, excuses for discipline, and fear for courage.

As you read these pages, you'll find my stories woven throughout, not because my life is extraordinary, but because they show what's possible when ordinary people commit to extraordinary standards. My hope is that these stories will spark something in you, challenge you, and most importantly, equip you to raise your own standards in whatever role you hold: parent, teacher, business owner, leader, or student.

The world doesn't get better by accident. It gets better because people like you decide to live better, lead better, and expect better. That is what it means to unleash your Level 10 life.

— James Theros

What Others Are Saying About Level 10 Martial Arts

"Dear Mr. and Ms. Theros,

The purpose of this letter is to inform you of the progress Noah has made since starting Martial Arts, and how it's helped him in so many areas.

Since starting with the program, Noah has shown so much progress in improving his grades. His teachers have noticed a huge change in him, and we have received so much positive feedback in the last few weeks. He has started coming home with A's, B's and C's, instead of some D's and F's we have seen before him joining, and every day has gotten better and better.

On the behavior and social aspect, Noah is showing a lot more focus and positive behaviors around his peers and teachers, as well as at home. He is becoming more and more responsible, and is taking more initiative in helping out around the house, completing his homework early and becoming more independent with his chores.

The change has been incredible, and we are so grateful we found your school. Every single instructor has been wonderful, and the environment is great.

Thank you for everything and we're looking forward to more great things to come!"

Sincerely,

—**Vanessa Landrum**

"A coworker and friend of mine encouraged me to get my 4 year old son involved in Tae Kwon Do. She had recently earned her black belt at Level 10 and knew that could help Ryan break out of his shell. He's always been a very shy and cautious child. He rarely spoke to other adults or children, regardless of whether he knew them or not. With Kindergarten quickly approaching, his daddy and I were worried about how he would handle it. We didn't want him to hide in the background and be afraid to interact with others.

Since starting, Ryan has grown in so many ways. He is more confident. He answers his teachers and myself with respect (yes/no ma'am). He is learning how to control his behavior in certain situations. And most importantly, he responds to others when spoken to (at least most of the time). We're still working at it, but now he will at least wave and smile in response; and to us, that is a huge accomplishment.

Ryan looks forward to going to class and seeing his friends. He has earned both his yellow and orange belt, and is about to earn his blue belt. After each test, I see such a feeling of accomplishment and pride on his face. Level 10 has definitely helped to bring Ryan out of his shell and I'm so glad that we got him involved!"

— **Kari Richardson**

"Level 10 Martial Arts College is an exceptional place. If you want a true personal and martial arts lifestyle change experience, WHAT ARE YOU WAITING FOR!!! Master and Mrs. Theros are exceptional people and leaders in Martial Arts and in the community.

They teach and mentor families in the true spirit of martial arts lifestyle. Master and Mrs. Theros have done nothing but given my family the utmost respect, and when we needed advice, or a simple kick in the backside to get back to focus, they have always been there.

They teach you to surround yourselves with successful people, positive thinking and positive role models so you too can be successful. From a martial arts skills standpoint, Master Theros and Mrs. Theros know their stuff. Our community needs more leaders like Master and Mrs. Theros.

What Others Are Saying About Level 10 Martial Arts

I want my daughter to go to a family friendly college, but one that teaches the upmost respect, self-discipline and traditional martial arts way of life. That's why we both train there!!! If I had the money to invest in another school and another city or state, I would be honored to be affiliated with Level 10 Martial Arts."

—Jack Reismiller (Group Executive VP of Business Improvement, Rolls Royce Corp)

"I can personally testify that if parents work to reinforce your lessons kids can be changed.

Brice's doctor wanted him placed on medication for attention deficit when he was in the 3rd grade. We chose Level 10 as an alternative. Four years later Brice has never been on medication, is a straight A student and manages to play football and baseball while continuing his training with you. He is not perfect by any means, but he is very focused on his goals of attending the Naval Academy and entering the Marines... not too shabby of a goal for a 7th grader. Brian and I attribute a lot of his success to you and your school.

He struggles sometimes with "needing a break," but he is always happy when we force him to stick it out. Parents need to understand that it is also their responsibility to instruct their children and that changes can't be made in just a couple hours a week at Level 10.

Even a year at training changed Allie. She was quiet and shy and lacked self confidence in herself. You would not believe the young lady she has become. She is now a junior at Franklin Central and is in her 3rd year of competition show choir. She performs on that stage like she owns the place and is very confident in herself... I attribute it to the first in-school competition she participated in when she won a gold medal. It was like a switch was flipped in how she viewed herself.

We appreciate everything you and Mrs. Theros have done for our family."

—Julie Clesi (mother of Brice and Allie)

"Martial Arts and Level 10 has been a positive part of my life. Since joining Level 10, my health, both mental and physical, has improved.

Before joining, I was always sick with colds and strep throat. My first and second grade years, I missed a lot of school for being sick. Since my first complete year at Level 10, I've had 1 year with perfect attendance and another with only 3 days missed. Physically, I feel I am doing great. I can do the full splits, kick a board above my head, and run more laps than most of the other boys at gym.

Mentally, I am able to concentrate better in class without day dreaming so much. Another positive effect, for joining Level 10, is that I am more confident. All of the students call me a nerd for always being able to answer questions. Before joining Level 10, I would never raise my hand to answer.

When my family was down, you helped us by showing that people do care. You welcomed me into the martial arts family and helped me become the young man I am today.

Thank you, Level 10 Rocks!"

— Matthew Seyler (Junior Black Belt, 11)

"Felicia was so shy and her self-confidence level was close to zero. She has now become such a champion in her leadership abilities that she came to the attention of United Way and is part of their teen leadership program and an ongoing volunteer.

Jordan has been struggling with ADHD since age 4. Kindergarten was terribly difficult for him and his focus and ability to sit still were

What Others Are Saying About Level 10 Martial Arts

zero percent. It amazed me how his training at Level 10 has brought out the best in him in school.

His teacher phoned me to say how well he is doing with the instrument. Felicia is in orchestra as well, playing violin. Who knew that Level 10 could give such a positive boost to the assist I needed in helping Jordan live successfully with ADHD!

Thank you, Level 10, for helping to make such a rewardingly positive influence a lifelong attribute in my grandchildren's lives!

—**Shirley Harris (Proud Grandmother)**

"Dear Master Theros,

It's amazing what you've done to my son. Wesley has always been a complicated kid. Honestly, before your class, I was talking to my husband about putting Wesley into counseling. I know this is probably hard to believe with how shy he is in your class, but it's true.

I really feel out of everyone participating Wesley has benefited the most. I wanted you to know what's been going on and Thank You for everything.

I'm so proud of Wesley."

—**Vanessa Mathias (Mother of Wesley, Age 7)**

"While in daycare, our son Daniel was signed up for a weekly Martial Arts class through Level 10. After a few months he came home and asked if he could start attending Level 10 at the school.

When we first started, it was not because of discipline or grades but because of how much fun he had learning the Martial Arts. As Daniel joined and promoted through the ranks, we have been able to directly leverage the skills of integrity, respect, perseverance, honesty, and indomitable spirit.

"Master Theros and the entire staff are excellent role models and have a true concern for the children in their care."

— **Dan Parker (Father of Daniel, Age 9)**

"Caden started at the age of 5 in the Little Ninja class and things have been going uphill since then for him.

I put Caden in martial arts when his dad and I were in the process of getting a divorce and it has helped him tremendously. I knew I was not going to be able to teach him all of the things he needed to learn as a young boy by myself. Level 10 has taught him respect, integrity, discipline, and self-control.

Now at age 10, he is a purple belt and on his way to being a black belt, which he is so excited about."

— **Lisa Shields (Mother of Caden, Age 10)**

"Last summer, Sabrina was in search of her identity as a growing young lady. We discovered that LTMA could be very beneficial to Sabrina and in the long run our family. We discovered that LTMA provided a great family atmosphere and attempted to find a way to help all who come to them.

Sabrina has been there for about 7 months now and things at home are improving. She has learned ways to cope with her siblings. She has improved in school as she has learned how to set goals, follow them, accomplish them, and enjoy the reward and satisfaction of completing them.

LTMA has provided her parents an opportunity to let her grow and mature in a structured environment. This provides so much for her that will affect her for the rest of her life. I don't believe she will ever forget this opportunity and neither will we her parents."

— **Edward and Lisa Cobb (Parents of Sabrina, Age 16)**

What Others Are Saying About Level 10 Martial Arts

"I cannot express how much it pleases me to tell you that Courtney, now nine, has achieved the goals that were set for her years ago.

She has never made any grade below an A. She has always been self-motivated but the teaching and instruction from Master Theros and his staff have reinforced that attitude. Courtney was so excited to be able to demonstrate her form and sparring in front of her class at school.

She was able to do so with a high degree of proficiency because of the work done at LTMA. She has also set a date to reach 2nd Dan Black Belt. I have no doubt she will accomplish this goal."

— David Hocutt (Father of Courtney, Age 10)

"This is not the first martial arts school our son has attended, but is, by far, the best. At Level 10, martial arts is not simply a sport, but a life choice.

Kicks and punches are not the most important things. Who our son is, as a human being, is as important to Master and Mrs. Theros as it is to us.

These two are interested and vested in our child and his future."

— Kara Doepker (Mother of Kyle, Age 10)

"When Rachel came home over 1 ½ years ago with a postcard from Level 10 to come try out two weeks of class, I wasn't quite sure what to think of her newfound interest and wondered just how long it would last. I actually put her off for a few weeks, but she kept on persisting on trying it out.

That was in January of 2006 and my husband and I have seen so many awesome changes in her. She immediately became hooked and pursued it with such a powerful spirit that we had never seen her exhibit…

We did experience a scare that no parent should ever have this past summer with a man that tried to abduct her. She smelled and sensed danger and ran and hid from the man. She hid and stayed quiet until he went away. I'm not so sure she would have handled this situation as well just two years ago.

She is still learning to be more responsible and self-sufficient. She has such wonderful support and great friends at Level 10 and it's like a second family for her and the rest of us.

Thanks to everyone for being part of Rachel's and our lives. God Bless."

— **Michelle Edmonds (Mother of Rachel, Age 9)**

"At a time where many are focused on the "art of fighting," Level 10 Martial Arts College seems to be more in line with "the art of peaceful living."

This school does not just focus on how to punch and kick (although we are taught very well), but how to be leaders in a society where one could argue that leadership is certainly lacking.

Honesty, modesty, loyalty, respect, and self-discipline are at the heart of EVERY lesson. This is a place where anyone can train...

My whole family is enrolled and it has only strengthened our family bond. The little ninja program is phenomenal, preparing young people for the world and teaching them safety concepts, confidence, self-discipline, self-control, and respect, all together with a fun workout...

This is a wonderfully innovative organization in the truest sense with awe-inspiring martial artists, but Master Theros' morality training secures its place on the "A List."

— **Shy-Quon Ely (Father of Daesjah, Age 9, and Darryn, Age 3)**

What Others Are Saying About Level 10 Martial Arts

"I enrolled in Level 10 Martial Arts College (LTMA) immediately after the formal orientation. I was thoroughly impressed and wanted to be very selective with choosing a school that fit my needs and met my high standards...

I have come to know LTMA as "my other family" and the strength, stamina, and discipline that I am gaining while in the school transfers to persistence, patience, and dedication needed in my professional and personal life.

I am much more confident, patient, diligent, motivated, humble, conscientious, loving, and stronger mentally, emotionally, physically, and spiritually.

The training that I continue to receive as I work to become a black belt is invaluable and I am blessed that there are people like Master and Mrs. Theros and our great teachers available to help me as I grow and mature as an individual and martial artist.

Becoming a student at Level 10 Martial Arts College has been one of the wisest decisions I have made in my 30+ years of living. I love my home away from home! Thanks LTMA family!"

— **Dr. Keema Cooper, 36 (Doctor of Internal Medicine)**

"You guys are great! Thank you for ALL YOU DO!! Everyone here has had such a huge impact on Kody. His self-esteem has improved a lot in the small amount of time we have been here.

Mr. Tucher and Ms. Fergason are personally responsible for encouraging Kody and helping him grow as a young man. He wants them to be proud of him and see what he can do.

All of the teachers and helpers here are pleasant, helpful, and most of all, a great influence on Kody and all the other students.

This school has the best group of people that help encourage, nurture, and push everyone to be the best they can be. But you welcome everyone like they are part of the family.

I would never want to go anywhere else but here after seeing how much he has changed. This school helps bring out the absolute best qualities in Kody.

In one sentence that covers it all... You Guys Rock!!"

— **Erin Finney (Mother of Kody, Age 12)**

"Level 10 provides a well-rounded martial arts education.

They focus on character building and leadership development, as well as the competitive, artistic, and self-defense aspects of the martial arts.

There are many good schools, but far too many are one-dimensional. Not Level 10.

They build black belts — from the inside out."

—**Jim Richards (Father of Nathan Richards, Black Belt, Age 16)**

"Level 10 Martial Arts has been a great experience for my 11-year-old son Thomas. He has gained confidence in himself, as well as learned how to control his emotions and channel anger in a healthy manner...

Level 10 Martial Arts gives children the tools they need to be successful in the world today. Thomas is recommended Black Belt now, and he takes great pride in knowing that when he receives his Black Belt, he has accomplished something that no other person can take from him.

More and more we hear on the news how Martial Arts training has helped someone or saved a life. Level 10 Martial Arts is a hands-down wonderful place for the whole family. When you walk *through the doors you can feel a sense of warmth, love, respect, and compassion — all attributes needed for survival in the uncertain world.*

Thomas made the 6th grade soccer team at his school. Two years ago he would not have even tried. For me as a parent that speaks volumes, how Martial Arts helps to mold children into responsible people, willing to take a chance and not afraid to fail, but learning how to try again.

HATS OFF TO LEVEL 10 MARTIALS ART, AND TO MASTER AND MRS. THEROS."

— **Theresa Barr (Mother of Thomas Barr, Age 10)**

"*Level 10 Martial Arts College has completely changed Tyler. Tyler was diagnosed with ADHD, his grades were average, he didn't want to do much of anything, was argumentative and could not control himself from getting into trouble...*

We started with Level 10 and Tyler knew within the first month he wanted to continue all the way to earn his Black Belt. He has learned so much more than Karate. He is now an honor roll student, has learned to set goals for himself, to believe in himself, to work hard to accomplish his goals, patience (with himself and others) and what it feels like to accomplish his goals.

He has more self-discipline, integrity, a healthy sense of self-confidence and self-esteem, respect for himself and others — and I have not received one phone call from the school regarding his behavior since he started!

Tyler looks up to Master Theros and ALL the other instructors and holds himself to a higher standard not only during classes but also at home and in school. I am very proud of who Tyler is and what choices and directions he now chooses for himself... It really is like a family and once your child starts coming here, he (she) will never want to leave."

— **Kimberly Lowe (Mother of Tyler, Age 10)**

"*I am very pleased with Level 10 and have talked your school up and will continue to do so to everyone I meet. It has been a wonderful place for Aaron and has helped him more than I (or his physical therapist) ever thought possible.*

What Level 10 has done for him though, is amazing. When he started, he couldn't balance on one foot or jump or skip. He still has trouble skipping but he is finally beginning to catch up to his peers physically.

I can't thank you enough for that. I hope you and Master Theros keep up the awesome work the two of you are doing and again I will be the first to say how wonderful Level 10 is."

—**Beth Roller (Mother of Aaron, Age 5)**

"*My son started at Level 10 after attending an amazing summer camp.*

I have tried for years to find something my son was passionate about and now I have finally found it at Level 10! After attending the school for about seven months, he still runs to get dressed for EVERY class and never complains when it's time to leave the house unlike other activities he has been involved in.

Maybe that is because Level 10 is not just another activity to keep him busy. Level 10 is a lifestyle and has changed him even in the short amount of time he has been there. His level of respect and regard for others has risen to a level I am VERY proud of! The difference in him is evident and his tuition is the only monthly bill I actually enjoy paying!!"

What Others Are Saying About Level 10 Martial Arts

—Julie Morgan (Mother of Connor Morgan, Age 10)

"Our 7-year-old son began martial arts in October and we have seen remarkable growth in him in areas we consider very important. He has more focus, dedication to completing tasks, and a mindset that he can do anything he sets his mind to.

We also like the strong emphasis on respect that Level 10 teaches. I thank Level 10 Martial Arts for encouraging the right values in addition to the physical training."

—Mindy Ashley (Mother of Travis, Age 7)

"I most definitely see a difference in my son Joshua since he has been a part of the L10 family. He helps out more at home without a fight, helps his little brother with making food, cleaning, etc., and listens better.

He doesn't talk back as much as he once did, and he doesn't get as agitated as he used to. I also see more focus when it comes time to practice at home. He has definitely changed for the better. I know as he works harder he will be even better as he grows.

I am very happy that he loves going to class and has fun doing it. I am very happy with the results of my son being a part of L10MA!"

— Melinda Rush (Mother of Joshua)

"A couple of weeks ago, Coner told us about an incident with a new boy in our neighborhood.

As he and a couple of other kids were trying to get on the bus, the new boy put his leg across the aisle to block Coner from going past. Coner asked him to move it and the boy ignored him. Coner jumped over his leg and went on about his business.

The next day the same situation arose but this time after the boy ignored Coner's request, Coner told him that if he did not remove his leg that he was going to hurt it. The boy continued to ignore him so Coner put his foot on the boy's knee and started to apply pressure. In Coner's words: "I didn't hardly push at all and he started screaming 'OUCH' and pulled his leg back."

Needless to say, he has had no further problems with this boy since. We don't feel this was the best way for him handle the situation but this is the first time Coner has stood up to anyone bullying him and we are very excited about that.

We could see the pride in his eyes while he told us the story. We want to thank you and all the Instructors that have worked so hard with him, his confidence in himself has improved dramatically since he started training at your school.

Thank you for all you do."

— **Nathan Chambers (Student and Father of Coner, Age 8)**

"Level 10 Martial Arts College of Palm Harbor, Florida is a family-oriented martial arts school and so much more.

Throughout the years, I have been able to see other martial arts facilities in our county by way of friends and their children. I have been very impressed with Level 10, from the first communication with Mrs. Theros, at the time we signed up our five-year-old granddaughter for classes. What we thought was going to be a six-week trial has grown into much more.

Our granddaughter absolutely loves Master Theros and Mrs. Theros, who have a gift for teaching what they have a passion for. However, karate is only a part of what is being taught. Life-long lessons, for both the student as well as the families, are taught in many ways. Respect, Focus, and Discipline are a major part of the learning and we, as a family, have seen this put into daily living practices.

What Others Are Saying About Level 10 Martial Arts

I have witnessed students working and achieving their goals through positive reinforcement, building their confidence, and learning as well as applying respect, focus, and discipline that they are taught. The relationships that the Theros have built with the students and families, along with the care that they give each and every one of them, is phenomenal.

Master and Mrs. Theros live up to their name and want all their students to achieve the same in their everyday life, in all they do by providing all the encouragement and tools they need. The owners of Level 10 Martial Arts College have provided an extremely clean, safe, and state-of-the-art facility that I would highly recommend to anyone."

— **Natalie Stephens (Palm Harbor, Florida)**

"I cannot thank you enough for the confidence you have instilled in Lennon over the past 6 months. Lennon used to shy away from other kids or take a while to warm up to them, but now he walks up to them with such confidence no matter their age.

It has been such a beautiful thing to watch as his mother. Thank you from the bottom of my heart."

— **Marna Osborne (Mother of Lennon)**

"On behalf of my husband and myself, I would like to say thank you for running a program that has helped our child grow and thrive. Since joining Level 10 Martial Arts, Bailey has gained more confidence in herself and has become more respectful of her parents, family members, and friends.

Bailey is also learning the value of hard work and practice and realizes she will not move forward in class and other areas of life without putting in the effort of studying at home and paying attention in class.

We appreciate and admire the owners and instructors greatly!"
— **Kayleigh Degen (Mother of Bailey Degen)**

"My name is Matt Tucher and I joined Level 10 Martial Arts in April of 2005. When I first started there, I got involved through the after school at South Grove Intermediate in Beech Grove and I fell in love instantly.

But I had a darker side of who I was when I was outside of LTMA and it was tearing me apart. I was very confused with a lot of what was happening in my life with my parents' divorce and I always got in fights with every single person in my life. Whether it was my mom or dad, my sister, grandparents, or friends, I was very hostile to them.

I was then sent to many doctors for medicine to make me less depressed and decrease my amount of anger towards anything and everything. Then one night after having a fight with my father behind our house in Beech Grove, he sent me to Valle Vista which is kind of like a mental hospital and rehabilitation center.

After going to LTMA and VV I became more respectful and happier. Coming to Level 10 and having Master Theros and all of the Instructors to help shape and change me as a person. It has allowed me to outgrow my shyness, lack of confidence, and depression of myself that I used to put myself through because I always thought I was unable to change my life and at some points in my life.

Since 2005 I have done many things I never thought I would ever get to: become confident, make friends, find a passion, change my weight problem, achieve and be a part of something HUGE, and help me change my life to graduate high school.

Everyday I get to walk into LTMA, teach students who are talented and eager to learn, then learn a very special art that my father and

I got to do together, and surround myself with special people and meet very famous stars and athletes.

I would have to say, without all of the support from the entire school and students there in my 8-year tenure there, I would either be in the mental house, in jail, or dead. That last statement was 100% true and I will believe that until the day I die. Level 10 saved my life and everyday I am thankful for Master Theros and his passion for martial arts and for helping people.

I love Level 10 Martial Arts with my whole heart. I'm Forever Thankful."

— Matt Tucher (5th Degree Black Belt)

"How wonderful to see the positive rewards of your program. Annie says, "Please and Thank you" without being reminded to do so. After being told to clean her room for homework, she came home and started on her assignment right away.

Not only did she clean her room, but she continued into her large walk-in closet. Annie has always been very shy. She never enjoyed any after school activities. We have signed her up for different afterschool programs, but she always changed her mind after the first visit.

We are so pleased that Annie enjoys your Martial Arts program. She is not shy in your class at all. My husband and I cannot get over her loud responses to your commands.

Television, Video games, NO MORE!! After school she practices her moves over and over. Whenever she is asked a question she answers "Yes Ma'am or No Ma'am" without hesitation.

We have three children, 15, 13 and 10. Anyone with three girls, close in age, knows the bickering that goes on over EVERYTHING!! The difference in the interaction between Annie and her sisters is wonderful. After using "please" and "thank you" when talking to her sisters, Annie has started a trend in our household. All of my children are using "Please" and "Thank you." Try putting a monetary value on that!!

The Martial Arts program is a wonderful gift for a child. Our children are being taught to handle a negative situation with positive life lessons.

School can be a scary place for our children at times. Your class teaches our children how to handle a negative confrontation from another student with positive skills that do not include fighting, name calling, or SCHOOL SUSPENSION!

With the dwindling activities at school, it is so wonderful to have a program we can allow our children to take part in."

— **Meredith and Jim Bryant (Parents of Annie Bryant, Indianapolis)**

"Dear Master Theros,

I wanted to share something with you and hope that you would share it with the Gold Team Leaders.

I had an interview today for a higher position at the college that I currently work at. I have only been here a few months but they were still willing to give me an interview for the position. During the entire interview he was asking me the standard questions you normally hear in an interview involving an office position. Then came the question of what do I do to help my "personal growth" and I answered him easily.

I told him that I have read self help books in the past and still have a few around that I go back to and reread the parts that I highlighted. The look on his face was priceless. He honestly looked taken back by my answer. He then asked me how old I was and I responded 21 and he said "and you read these types of books?" and I said yes.

What Others Are Saying About Level 10 Martial Arts

I told him that I have been in a Leadership Program for over 7 years and have read books like these for the past few years. I also mentioned the trip to Florida we all took back in Sept of 2008 and all the speakers I was able to hear and learn from.

The reason for this email is to thank you for having me read those books and influencing me in a positive way and steering me in the right direction. I received a second interview on the spot. I highly believe that because I have read those books, it helped me receive the second interview next week.

I am blessed and very thankful for everything that you have done for me in Martial Arts and in my life.

Forever your student"
— **Ashley Furgason (5th Degree Black Belt)**

"When I first stepped on the mat at Level 10 Martial Arts as a student, I had no idea how my life was about to change. At the age of 38, I was nearly 70 pounds heavier than I wanted to be... and so physically challenged I was not sure I could make it through the warm-ups, let alone the rest of class!

But for the better part of a year, I had sat on the sidelines watching. First I watched my oldest son in class. A few months later my youngest began training, followed immediately by my husband. When Dad joined our sons on the mat, our sons' happiness was clearly visible and training together managed to strengthen an already strong father-sons bond.

My family very much wanted me to join them. But still I held back, allowing my fear of embarrassment and failure to control me. My fear kept me static, but my interest continued to grow, because Tae Kwon Do looked like so much fun! Continued encouragement from my family, the instructors, and other students finally led me to agree.

My husband and I had wanted our children to join martial arts to increase their confidence and help them learn self-control. We had very specific ideas about what we wanted in a martial arts school and were thrilled with what we found at Level 10 because students learn not only how to defend themselves, but more importantly they learn principles that help them avoid situations that would necessitate using what they have learned. Every lesson stresses the principles of focus, self-discipline, confidence, respect and persistence.

These principles are demonstrated by the instructors, taught through the martial arts skills and discussed repeatedly in class. The classes are structured to teach martial arts skills while also teaching you how to live your life as a confident, respectful leader.

Ironically, before I started my training, it did not occur to me that those principles could benefit me. It was my desire to improve myself physically that led me to the mat. But what keeps me there today is how Level 10 has changed me mentally and emotionally.

Yes, I have lost much of the weight, and my physical skills continue to improve. But more significant is that I have changed from the frightened person with a lifelong fear of embarrassing herself, into a much more confident woman who understands that I am going to make mistakes and I am likely to embarrass myself, but that it does not matter. Part of my growth has been realizing that each mistake takes me one step closer to being the kind of person I have always dreamed of being!

Along the way I find myself in class with people who encourage and are willing to give a hand to anyone who is struggling. Nowhere else in life have I experienced the true essence of "team spirit" like I do in this sport that is supposedly geared to the individual. Discipline and hard work are expected, but success, at whatever level, is celebrated.

At this point in my training I am halfway to my first black belt and am already forever changed. I am learning to step out of my comfort zone, and meet challenges. I am learning leadership skills that are invaluable in my life "off the mat". That is the core of training at Level 10—learning principles that make you a better person when you walk out of the door at the end of each lesson.

At the beginning of my training, I could not imagine myself earning a black belt. However, I have evolved. I am no longer the woman I was, physically or mentally. As I look down the road, I believe I will earn my black belt. It is exhilarating to know that along the way I will continue to grow and evolve in positive ways that will enable me to set and accomplish goals, both on and off the mat. I know the woman who earns that black belt will not be the one who stepped on the mat the first day, or even the woman I am today, and I look forward to becoming her!"

— **Barb Lawson**

"My name is Chris York and I have been a Level 10 student for a year and 3 months.

My wife and I enrolled our son as a student after he expressed an interest in learning martial arts. Level 10 was close to home, had good reviews and had a great introductory special for new students, so we thought "what do we have to lose?"

He ended up loving it immediately and has been a student for just short of 2 years now.

I first stepped out onto the mat during a Father's Day "Dad's Train Free" special offer. I was hooked immediately as well. At 41 years old, I had some serious doubts about whether this is something I should be doing to myself.

Now I'm in just as good, if not better shape than I was as a teenager. At Level 10 it's not all about the physical aspects of martial arts, they stress the mental gains as well. Respect, confidence, self-discipline and focus.

I personally have benefitted greatly in my confidence level. The boost in my self-confidence is pretty amazing to see when comparing where I'm at now in my training and how I was as a new student.

The instructors and staff are all professional, courteous and have a genuine love of teaching martial arts. They strive to create a family friendly environment and are very successful at it. If you have children, get them into Level 10.

The physical and mental training they'll receive is the perfect way to help them be successful in life. If you're an adult such as myself, get into Level 10. I am proof that it's never too late to improve yourself and have a great time doing it as well!"

— **Chris York**

"*I just wanna say that, even though my son, Graham, has only been doing martial arts for about three weeks, the improvement in his attitude has been priceless. He calls me yes ma'am at home, he helped me twice this week without me even asking. He helped me carrying groceries and clean the kitchen while I was making dinner. I am so proud and more than anything, he seems proud of himself already and strives to earn the next stripes. I cannot wait to continue watching his confidence and respect bloom. Debi and Grand Master James are absolutely incredible with the kids (and adults) and I can't recommend Level 10 Martial Arts enough!"*

— **Amy Perkett**

"My boys has flourished both mentally and physically since starting Level10 a few months ago. The instructors are a perfect blend of warmth and assertiveness, creating a nurturing yet structured environment. They instill confidence and discipline in every class, helping to develop a strong sense of self and respect for others. The positive atmosphere and focused teaching style have truly made a difference in my children's growth. Highly recommend for anyone looking to build their kid's character and skills!"

—**Samantha Grant**

"All the instructors teach basic good morals and proper techniques. Fair and honest ways to learn winning and losing. Everyone learns. I can't share the impact this school has made on our family! Thank you. All of Level 10 College Martial Arts… The BEST."

—**Tracy Toombs**

"Level 10 is more than just a place to send your child to learn martial Arts it's a family. My child has been going now for 2 years and I can see positive changes in him. His confidence and coordination have improved. I can't say enough positive things about the program and the owners. They go above and beyond. Your child learns so much more than martial arts — they will learn life lessons, how to be leaders all while having fun."

— **Genevieve Calhoun**

"Level 10 Martial Arts College has been life changing for me. It has helped me gain a lot of confidence, strength, endurance, discipline, determination, and so much more great qualities. I have been attending Level 10 Martial Arts College for about 4 years and the skills that I have are some thing that I am very proud of. One of the programs that I'm in is called Leadership. Leadership helps me obtain not just Martial Art skills but real world skills too. I 100% recommend this to you or your child."

— **Abraham Lizano**

"We signed up our 5 year old granddaughter for a 6 week trial, thinking it would give her something fun to do. What we didn't expect was this same 5 year old little girl that loves her newfound martial arts family and all that is learning. Her confidence, discipline, respect, skills and focus have amazed us. She has been attending for almost 6 months and Master Theros and Instructor Mrs. Theros truly care for their students of all ages and are teaching far more than karate martial arts!! As a woman of faith, we are blessed to have found Level 10, with a wonderful foundation and values that they show in the way they live and instruct!!"

— **Natalie Stephens**

"This school has helped my son improve in confidence and gain focus and perseverance. They work hard at building a community for the students and families."

— **Elizabeth Cameron**

"My 7 year old Lewis is in his 4th semester with Level 10 Martial Arts College. He is learning the importance of confidence, patience and respect. As well as, self defense. He made a testimonial video but I'm only seeing where photos can be posted not videos. But he said his confidence has improved, he has more patience and he's working towards his black belt. I would highly recommend Level 10 Martial Arts College to anyone wanting to better themselves or their child. Lewis is wrapping up his 5th semester. He has joined the Leadership team and is learning to help other students improve their skills. He's loving it!"

— **Kathy Queensberry**

"L10 has been an amazing place for my son to grow into a focused and disciplined young man. It has boosted his confidence, along with improving his physical abilities. He is challenged to meet high stands

while having fun in a positive and safe environment. There are many basic life lessons that are taught at L10 that are essential to being a successful person in life and I am thankful to have my son involved."
— **Katrina Cottrell**

"Mr and Mrs Theros are inspiring martial arts teachers. Beyond teaching a top notch Karate curriculum, their school is a family oriented environment and provides kids and adults with a positive mindset, discipline, respect, kindness in practice. They lead by example and older kids are taught to help and support younger ones. We've had our 6 yr old son here for almost 2 years, he's progressing very well and all of us love it. Couldn't recommend it more!"
— **Maisa Roberts**

"If you are looking for a place for your child(ren) to learn, understand, and put into practice patience, respect, honesty, modesty, and discipline all while learning Tae Kwon Do, Level 10 Martial Arts is the best school in Pinellas County. (Personally I think anywhere) We have looked at and enrolled in several others. Even better, you can join with your kids and get an amazing workout while learning something new and bonding with your child. Thank you Master and Mrs Theros for building this community, and Mrs. Manning for all you have done to encourage us as we have begun our journey!"
— **Candice Bakke**

"Level 10 Martial Arts is a great place to learn focus respect and discipline. Our two young boys started at the age 4 and 6. They have been attending the last three years! It has helped them develop social and personal skills as well as their martial arts skills. Level 10 has become a second family, we have met some really great students and teachers. I would recommend this to everyone. I am

most impressed with how they treat the students and hold them to account for their own behaviors and responsibilities."
—**Tom Dawe**

"If you are looking for a great way to get your kid away from the computer screen and build their confidence, this martial arts school would be a great character and confidence builder for your child. Once you walk through that door, you can see and feel the positive energy that's inside."
—**Klaris Dauti**

"Level 10 Martial Arts College has impacted my life in many ways. I've developed confidence, patience, discipline, and much more over these past years. As well as focus and respect. I've also developed much more strength. My public speaking skills have also gotten much better through the leadership program. I also have made many great friends at L10. L10 has brought so much joy to my life, and attending class always helps take my mind off things. I highly recommend joining Level 10 Martial Arts College, you'll never regret it."
—**Melissa McBride**

"I think karate has helped me a lot more with my confidence, and I feel like I've gotten a lot more responsible doing karate. Thank you."
—**Vincent Reale**

We started at level 10 when Adrian was three. His first couple classes he could barely stand still without wiggling and dancing and looking around. All we heard was Adrian Focus, Adrian. He required a lot of help at first, but slowly he started to be able to stand and focus without as much help from the assistance.

What Others Are Saying About Level 10 Martial Arts

His teacher at daycare even told me that she would see him in class and he would practice standing at attention. When he got his belt, he was so excited and as he started to move up and rank, he became more confident and he would ask to practice without me having to tell him. He gets excited about.

Being able to compete and he's able to accept not winning every time without getting upset. I'm amazed at how much he has grown in such a short time and I can't wait to see the growth that is ahead of him. They say that it takes a village to raise a kid, and I am very blessed to be able to call level 10 part of my village.

—Mariana Reyes

My son, Aidan Osborne, has been attending Level 10 martial Arts for just about three years now, and I have.

Martial arts for just about three years now, and I have enjoyed every moment of it. We are having a lot. My son, Aidan Osborne, has been attending Level 10 martial Arts for just about three years now, and I have enjoyed every moment of it. We were having a lot of behavior and educational problems when it came to Aiden, but ever since he has started, his confidence has increased tremendously.

He takes pride in what he does in school and at home. He also, his behavior also has become. More stable. I would get a lot of phone calls regarding aid and run outta class and not completing his work. He does not do that anymore, so I'm so grateful. I'm so grateful for what Level 10 has offered and provided my son.

I wouldn't change it for the world. It is an awesome place."

—Dominique Osborne

"*My son Andrew, has been going there for a little bit over two years. Andrew has a diagnosis of Global Apraxia, which is a neurological disorder that affects his small and fine and gross motor skills. Karate has been instrumental in helping him to improve his coordination and that in turn has helped his self-confidence.*

His teachers are always saying how he's much, much better at self advocating, and he goes over, above and beyond any expectations that they have for him. And that's because level 10 Martial Arts College truly instills a sense of higher standards, higher expectations. Grandmaster gives much more than just martial arts instruction.

He gives them life lessons that they can take with them well after their time at his school. Um, he's also really awesome at getting other instructors and other grand masters to come and give his students experiences that they just wouldn't get at any other school that are absolutely priceless. Um. The whole school is a community as well."

—Genevieve Calhoun

"Ever since our daughter, Isabella Campo has been going to Level 10, we've seen such a change in her. She's been more responsible. She has taken on to do more. Ever since she's been going there, it's also given us peace of mind, or it's given me peace of mind that she's been able to know and learn self-defense, something that I thought all young ladies should have, and I just think that.

The way she's been taught there. It has just really been peace of mind to me and my family, knowing that she's always taken care of and it's just always been such a great thing to be part of it with her.

At first when she started doing it, she's never been into sports and she's just changed, inside and out. I'm eternally grateful. Thank you very much."

—Steve Campo

What Others Are Saying About Level 10 Martial Arts

"In the 36 years that I've been in and out of martial arts, I've been in a few quality programs, but level 10 is absolutely the best. The other ones would teach quality skills, they could win tournaments, that sort of thing. But I don't ever remember them trying to teach us to be better people. Grandmaster has mentioned in the past few years ago that his real goal is to make better people.

Never really heard that in the other martial arts, but in the same sense, we also tend to win tournaments, so we are getting both being better people and the skills it takes to win. The other thing is, is that the people of Level 10 were a family and. It is just better quality people that are in this particular martial arts.

"When I first started, my husband had mentioned, yeah, your confidence is better. I didn't see it. Grandmaster agreed, he thought it was better. A few years later I did start to notice that my confidence was getting better.

I like myself a whole lot better than I used to. The pushing out of the comfort zone is really, I think, what gets us to that point

I'm not as afraid of being afraid anymore. And let's face it, being in your comfort zone is boring. I'd like to recommend that, once you become a black belt, once you take the first black belt test, don't stop. Because I am finding after taking those first couple black belt tests that going into my next black belt test, the confidence is up.

Through experience, I can say this is the best program I've ever been in. It's absolutely the best people that I've ever been in with martial arts and we also have Grandmaster who was National champion for years, has been teaching for well over 25 years.

You're gonna be hard pressed to find that kind of quality anywhere else. Thanks."

—**Chris Manning**

"I have so many wonderful things to say about Level 10 Martial Arts College. As a 64-year-old female just starting out in a program there, I have had so much positive reinforcement. Age doesn't matter. We all suffer the same things. Initially I started the program to lose weight, maintain, and to just move around.

I had tried gyms and yoga and different things. None of it was for me. I checked around different schools and I chose this one. It is not the nearest one to my home, but it, I liked the sound of their program.

I also do like the fact that they do pull you out of your comfort zone. At times, it is a little bit uncomfortable to be called on suddenly, and it takes me back to my days in school where I suddenly panic and oh my gosh, I can't do that. But over the months I've learned. Not to have the negative attitude of, I can't, I work really hard at pushing myself to know that I can do this, and they take into consideration age as well.

I highly recommend level 10 for any age!

—**Esther Aponte**

"Level 10 Martial Arts has helped me in so many ways. Before martial arts, I had a hard time focusing on what the teachers were teaching, and I got distracted very easily causing bad grades. It was also hard to avoid bumping into other students while moving to the next class because it is very crowded now.

After practicing martial arts for almost a year, I am a lot more focused than before.

My grades are all As and Bs. And I am now able to avoid bumping into other students in the halls. I'm also a lot more confident and less shy around people than I used to be. Classes at Level 10 martial arts are challenging and a lot fun.

What Others Are Saying About Level 10 Martial Arts

I've also learned a lot of important lessons. Like the seven phrases of respect. Yes, sir. Yes ma'am. No, sir. No ma'am. Please thank you and you're welcome. I've also learned about discipline by always doing the right thing by doing, by always doing what the instructors tell me. And I've learned that it's important to do the right thing because it is the right thing to do.

Even when, no, even when nobody is watching this, this has helped me even at home to be more respectful to my parents and grandparents.

I'm so happy that my parents signed me up for martial arts."

—Jack Blackburn

"Level 10 has helped me improve my strength, sincerity, flexibility, discipline, and respect, and I'm more kinder and nicer to my friends now because of level 10."

—Jonah Brenay

"I've noticed lately that I've had a more positive mindset when I go into serious situations. When it comes down to a serious matter, I've noticed that instead of thinking negatively right away, I think positively.

I've noticed that my health actually has been a lot better, especially in my mental, my physical health. I've always struggled with my weight when I was growing up, and it's always been like an obstacle that I would have to overcome. And I, when I joined Karate, it all started becoming better. I started feeling happier and excited for new things to happen.

I've also noticed my flexibility and my strength has improved a lot. I was always flexible anyways because I've been in cheerleading and all these other sports, but joining martial arts has really helped my flexibility. And I'm really glad that I'm starting to be happier. I'm starting to think more positive instead of negative."

—Josi Edwards

"I must say that the moment I walked in the door and I had a chat with Debi Theros and with Grand Master, Theros, I felt like I, they were family.

I felt so welcome. And I knew that I could put the most important charge of my life, which is the growth and development of my grandson. I felt very comfortable doing it, and I've been very pleased ever since. We've been a member of the Level 10 family for a couple years now, and it's just been a joy.

I also see that like to see Jude learning the lessons, trying to practice and stay focused, and there's a lot of life lessons that are taught at Level 10. It's not just that you show up and people kick each other and fight each other. That's not what Level 10 is all about.

I've learned this because I've seen the classes. It's really about learning self-discipline, and there's a spiritual thing about that, that it was hard to understand that I'm beginning to understand more and more as the years go by.

—Tim Shack (Grandfather of Jude)

"We were looking for an activity for Rose, and we had looked it around at a couple different options. We were thinking about gymnastics or dance, and we also thought about martial arts. When we looked at the option of martial arts, it was like, well, we can take rose to gymnastics and sit there and be bored and read a book and watch her having fun and work with her at home.

Or, all of us could do martial arts as a family activity and we decided to give it a try. And once we started kicking together, we were just sticking together and we just loved it.

There's a reason to be here.

The reason is, is that the physical is not the only benefits. There are lots of benefits that aren't physical that you can learn on this floor no matter what. The confidence, the self esteem, the ability to understand that it doesn't matter if you fail that only through failure do we really find out who we are.

—Robert Bollerman

1

The Silent Enemy, Mediocrity

Mediocrity is a thief.

It rarely storms into your life with a loud crash. It doesn't demand your attention or threaten you directly. Instead, it slips in quietly, disguised as comfort, disguised as safety, disguised as *"good enough."* It whispers in your ear, *"You've already done a lot today, take it easy."* Or, *"Why push yourself harder? Nobody will notice anyway."*

At first, it feels harmless. Who doesn't want to be comfortable? Who doesn't want to avoid unnecessary struggle? But mediocrity has one agenda: to keep you average, to rob you of your potential, and to make sure you never discover what you're truly capable of.

I know this enemy well.

Five Years in the Same Belt

I spent five long years stuck at the same rank of purple belt. Five years tying the same belt around my waist, watching others pass me by, convincing myself that maybe martial arts just wasn't meant for me.

But the truth was, it wasn't my instructor holding me back. It wasn't bad luck. It wasn't even my circumstances. It was me.

I let distractions win. Instead of showing up to class consistently, I let breakdancing and teenage fun steal my focus. I moved back and forth between Indiana and Minnesota, which made it harder to stay steady. But even when I had opportunities to train, I didn't take full advantage of them.

I told myself I'd get serious *tomorrow*. I'd focus *next month*. I'd put in the work *later*.

Later turned into years.

What I didn't realize back then is that mediocrity is rarely about a single bad choice, it's about small compromises repeated over time. Skipping one class doesn't make you mediocre. But skipping ten, then twenty, then fifty? That's when the "purple belt" becomes more than a rank. It becomes a lifestyle.

When I finally decided to stop giving in to mediocrity, I discovered something powerful: it wasn't talent I was missing, it was consistency.

Mediocrity Is Everywhere

My purple belt story might sound specific to martial arts, but mediocrity doesn't care what arena you're in, it shows up everywhere.

- Parents slip into mediocrity when they stop modeling the very behaviors they want their kids to adopt. They say, *"Be respectful,"* but yell at the server when their order is wrong. They say, *"Work hard,"* but their kids never see them commit to anything difficult themselves.

- Teachers fall into mediocrity when they lower expectations for their students, accepting half-effort because it's easier than pushing kids to their best.

- Business owners give into mediocrity when they play small, sticking with what feels safe instead of innovating, risking, and growing.

The Silent Enemy, Mediocrity

- Students settle into mediocrity when they choose comfort over discipline, scrolling on their phones instead of studying, or skipping practice because it's easier to stay home.

If we're honest, we've all been there. Mediocrity is appealing because it's easy. But here's the truth: mediocrity always costs more than excellence.

Excellence demands sweat, focus, and sacrifice up front. Mediocrity makes you pay later, with regret.

Three Faces of Mediocrity

Over the years, I've come to see mediocrity in three main disguises:

1. **Comfort**
   Comfort tells you to avoid the hard road. It convinces you that pain is bad and ease is good. The problem? All growth lives outside your comfort zone. Comfort keeps you small.

2. **Distraction**
   Distraction doesn't usually look harmful, it looks fun, exciting, even productive. But distraction steals your focus from what matters most. My years of breakdancing weren't evil, but they distracted me from my greater goal.

3. **Fear**
   Fear whispers, *"What if you fail?"* And sometimes, mediocrity feels safer than risk. But choosing mediocrity to avoid failure is the fastest way to guarantee it.

If you want to live a Level 10 life, you have to learn to recognize these disguises, and reject them.

A Conversation with Parents

Parents sometimes ask me, "*Why should I push my child so hard? Isn't it enough that they're just doing something positive?*"

I get it. Nobody wants to see their child struggle. But here's the truth: when you allow your child to quit whenever something gets difficult, you're not protecting them, you're training them to settle. You're teaching them that mediocrity is acceptable.

Children don't learn resilience by coasting. They learn it by facing something hard, failing at it, and then trying again. When you hold them accountable to finish what they start, even when it's uncomfortable, you're teaching them how to win the fight against mediocrity.

The Business Owner's Trap

I've been there myself. For the first six years of running my martial arts school, I struggled financially because I didn't know what I was doing. Instead of humbling myself to learn, I told myself things like, "*We're doing okay,*" or "*As long as the doors are open, that's enough.*"

That was mediocrity talking.

Eventually, I had to invest thousands of dollars into mentorship and education. I traveled across the country and around the world to train. I swallowed my pride and admitted I needed help.

That decision transformed my business, my teaching, and my life. Excellence wasn't optional, it was survival.

For Students

If you're a student, mediocrity often looks like giving the bare minimum. Maybe you know you could push harder in practice, but you don't. Maybe you settle for a C when you know you're capable of a B or an A. Maybe you let others think you're lazy because you'd rather be "cool" than be excellent.

Here's what I wish I could go back and tell my purple-belt self:

Mediocrity feels safe now, but it will rob you later. Push now, and you'll thank yourself for decades to come.

Level 10 Takeaways

- Consistency beats talent. It's not what you do once in a while, but what you do daily that defines your life.
- Mediocrity is sneaky. It doesn't look dangerous, but it kills dreams quietly.
- Excellence is a choice. Every day, you can choose focus over distraction, persistence over quitting.
- Your example matters. Whether you're a parent, teacher, leader, or student, others are watching how you handle mediocrity.

> ## PRACTICAL EXERCISES
>
> 1. Spot the Comfort Zone: Write down one area where you've been coasting. Where have you settled for "good enough"?
>
> 2. Identify the Disguise: Is mediocrity showing up as comfort, distraction, or fear in that area? Be honest with yourself.
>
> 3. Set a Standard: Decide what "Level 10" looks like in that area. Is it showing up three times a week? Is it putting away your phone while working? Is it leading with more patience?
>
> 4. Take Action This Week: Choose one small step to replace mediocrity with excellence, and commit to it.

Mediocrity will always be there, waiting for you. It doesn't leave. But neither does excellence. Both are available every single day. The question is, which one will you choose?

In the next chapter, we'll look at one of the greatest weapons against mediocrity: resilience. Because if you're going to live a Level 10 life, you have to learn how to fall down, and more importantly, how to get back up again.

2

Fall Down 7 Times, Get Up 8

There's an old Japanese proverb: *"Fall down seven times, get up eight."*

On paper, it looks simple. Just keep getting up. But anyone who has ever tasted failure knows that standing up again is rarely easy. Failure stings. Disappointment is heavy. Quitting feels easier.

And yet, it's this one simple habit, getting up one more time, that separates those who live at Level 10 from those who stay stuck at average.

Eight Years of Losing

When I think about resilience, my mind immediately goes back to my tournament years. For eight long years, I competed in event after event without winning the top prize. Eight years of driving to competitions, paying the fees, training hard, and still walking away empty-handed.

Do you know how discouraging it is to show up year after year, giving everything you've got, and still losing? It would have been easy, logical even, to quit. Plenty of people did.

But for some reason, I kept showing up. Something in me believed that if I just kept stepping onto the mat, if I just kept working, if I just kept standing back up after every loss, eventually, I'd break through.

And eventually, I did.

When Persistence Paid Off

The first time I finally placed in a competition, I didn't walk away with a giant trophy or a shiny medal, I walked away with a handwritten certificate for 5th place…in a division of six competitors. To anyone else, it might not have seemed like much, but to me, it felt like a mountain climbed. It was the first time I wasn't last.

That moment laid the foundation for what came later. Years down the road, when I won my first traditional grand champion award, the victory carried the weight of every small step before it. But what made it powerful wasn't just the title, it was what followed.

A Chinese master sat down beside me and said, "I've never seen someone show such power in a form before." That meant more than the medal around my neck. At another event, a Korean master told me he'd never forget me because of the way I performed my forms and weapons. And then there was the compliment that still makes me smile: "You're starting to look like your Master." That one touched me deeply, because more than anything, I wanted to reflect the example my teacher set.

None of those compliments, none of those victories, would have meant anything without the years of losing first. Without failure, the recognition would have felt hollow. But because of where I started, even a 5th-place certificate mattered. And it made every triumph after that feel all the richer.

The Hidden Gift of Losing

Most people avoid losing at all costs, but losing has gifts that winning can't give.
- Losing strips away ego. You can't fake success. Losing forces humility.
- Losing forces evaluation. You ask yourself, *"What am I missing? What can I do better?"*
- Losing develops empathy. You understand others who struggle, which makes you a more compassionate leader, teacher, or parent.
- Losing makes victory meaningful. Success without struggle feels shallow. Success after struggle feels unforgettable.

The truth is, the eight years of losing shaped me more than any of my victories ever could.

Resilience in Daily Life

You don't have to be a martial artist to need resilience. Life will knock you down in dozens of ways:
- **Parents:** Maybe your child is struggling with grades or behavior, and it feels like you're failing no matter what you do. Standing back up means staying consistent in your love and discipline, even when it's exhausting.
- **Teachers/Coaches:** Students will disappoint you. Some will quit. Some will test your patience. Resilience is showing up the next day, ready to teach again with the same energy and care.

- **Business Owners:** Plans collapse, staff leave, sales dip. Resilience is refusing to let a bad month, or even a bad year, define the future of your business.
- **Students:** Maybe you fail a test, lose a game, or get embarrassed in front of others. Resilience is not letting that failure become your identity. It's choosing to try again.

Resilience is not a trait you're born with. It's a muscle you build every time you stand back up.

How to Build Resilience

1. Expect the Fall
Failure isn't a possibility, it's a guarantee. Once you accept that, you stop being surprised when it happens.

2. Shorten the Gap
The quicker you get back up, the stronger you become. Don't let a failure keep you down for days or weeks. Bounce back faster each time.

3. Redefine Failure
Failure isn't final. It's feedback. Every loss is telling you something, if you're willing to listen.

4. Anchor in Purpose
If your "why" is strong enough, you'll always find the strength to rise again. For me, I wanted to honor my teacher and prove to myself that mediocrity wouldn't win.

A Word to Parents

I've seen well-meaning parents rescue their children from every failure. They step in when the child struggles, they soften the discipline when the child protests, they remove the obstacles so the child doesn't stumble.

But here's the hard truth: every time you shield your child from falling, you rob them of the chance to practice standing back up. Resilience isn't learned by being rescued, it's learned by recovering.

If you want your child to live a Level 10 life, let them fail sometimes. Then teach them how to get back up.

A Word to Teachers and Leaders

You will face students who disappoint you. Employees who let you down. Athletes who don't perform. Resilience for a leader is the willingness to keep showing up, keep believing, and keep pushing forward, even when others give up.

Your resilience becomes their model.

Level 10 Takeaways

- Resilience is built, not born. Every time you rise, you strengthen it.
- Compliments mean more after struggle. Recognition carries weight when it's earned through persistence.
- Losing is training in disguise. Failure refines you more than success.
- Your example of resilience inspires others. Parents, teachers, leaders, people are watching how you handle setbacks.

PRACTICAL EXERCISES

1. Identify a Fall: Write down one recent setback or failure you've experienced.
2. Evaluate: Ask yourself, *"What is this failure teaching me?"*
3. Shorten the Gap: Decide how quickly you'll rise next time. Don't let a setback keep you down longer than it should.
4. Teach It: Share a personal story of resilience with someone younger (a child, student, or employee). Let them see that standing back up is normal.

Resilience isn't glamorous. It's not the stuff of highlight reels. But it's the quiet strength that carries you through.

Fall down seven times, get up eight. That's not just a proverb. It's the way you win against mediocrity.

3

The Power of Role Models

When people look back on their lives, they rarely remember every detail of what their teachers or parents *said*. What they remember is how those people *lived*.

The truth is, whether you realize it or not, you are always on stage. Someone, your child, your student, your employee, your friend, is watching you. They're learning from your actions, not just your words. They're absorbing your habits, your attitude, your resilience, and your standards.

That realization changed everything for me.

Compliments That Hit Different

I've received trophies, medals, and awards over the years. They're nice, but they gather dust. What sticks with me are the compliments that pointed not to my skills, but to my example.

One of the greatest came after a competition when a master approached me and said, *"You're starting to look like your Master."*

That statement touched me more deeply than any award could, because it meant I was reflecting the influence of the person who had given so much to me. My Master's teaching wasn't just in my technique, it was in my demeanor, my attitude, my presence. And to hear that I was beginning to resemble him wasn't just praise; it was a reminder that I had a responsibility to carry on his example.

At another competition, after I performed, a Chinese master sat down beside me and said he had never seen someone show such power in a form before. Later, a Korean master told me he would never forget me because of the way I performed my forms and weapons at his event.

But perhaps the most meaningful compliments have not been about me at all, they've been about my students and families. At tournaments, people often tell me how impressed they are with our team's respect, humility, and sportsmanship. While other schools sometimes get caught up in ego or poor behavior, ours has built a reputation for integrity. Parents, coaches, and judges notice it. That reputation is the fruit of a culture we've built intentionally at my school, and it reminds me that being a role model isn't just personal, it's cultural.

The Role Model Multiplier

Here's what I've learned: being a role model multiplies. One person's example doesn't just impact one life; it ripples outward.

- Parents: Your children may not always listen to what you say, but they are always imitating what you do. If you handle conflict with anger, don't be surprised when they do the same. If you model respect, even in small interactions, they will learn to carry respect with them.
- Teachers and Coaches: Your students are absorbing your habits. If you cut corners, they'll cut corners. If you demand discipline but don't practice it yourself, they'll see the gap. But if you consistently show patience, respect, and focus, they'll carry those values long after they forget your lessons.
- Business Leaders: Your employees reflect your standards. If you slack off, so will they. If you gossip, they'll gossip. But if you show up early, stay consistent, and treat people with fairness, your culture will reflect it.

- Students: Even if you think nobody notices you, younger students do. They're watching how you train, how you behave, and how you handle pressure. You are a role model whether you accept it or not.

Being a role model isn't optional, it's automatic. The question isn't *"Am I a role model?"* The question is, *"What kind of role model am I?"*

Why Role Models Matter

In a world where mediocrity is common and negativity spreads fast, role models matter more than ever.

Kids don't need more celebrities to copy. They need real-life heroes, parents, teachers, coaches, who show them what character looks like. Employees don't need bosses who preach vision but live by convenience; they need leaders who embody the culture they claim to value. Students don't need lectures on perseverance; they need examples of it.

The best role models aren't perfect, they're consistent. They're not flawless; they're faithful. People don't need you to never stumble; they need to see that when you do stumble, you stand back up and keep moving forward.

Culture Is Caught, Not Taught

At my school, I teach respect, focus, and discipline as core values. But the truth is, my students don't just *learn* those values, they *catch* them by watching the example set by instructors, leaders, and parents.

That's why our school is known for humility and respect at tournaments. It's not because we hand out a rule sheet; it's because our students see those values modeled in every class. They see their instructors bowing with sincerity, treating others kindly, and holding themselves to a high standard. Over time, they begin to live out those same behaviors.

This is true in families, businesses, and classrooms, too. The culture you want can't just be taught; it has to be modeled. People don't just hear what you say, they copy what you live.

The Responsibility of Influence

Being a role model is both a privilege and a responsibility. You never know who is watching you. It could be your child, your student, a stranger at the grocery store, or an employee in a meeting. One moment of integrity, or one moment of compromise, can shape how they view you, and sometimes, how they view themselves.

That's a heavy responsibility. But it's also one of the greatest opportunities you'll ever have.

Level 10 Takeaways

- Example is louder than words. People copy what you *do*, not what you say.
- Consistency builds credibility. Compliments and recognition are born from steady example, not occasional effort.
- Culture grows from leaders. The standards you live by become the standards of your family, classroom, or business.
- You're always a role model. The only question is: are you a good one?

> **PRACTICAL EXERCISES**
>
> 1. Mirror Test: Look at your day honestly and ask, "*Would I want someone I care about to copy the way I lived today?*"
> 2. Identify Your Gap: Write down one area where your words and actions don't match. For example, do you tell your kids not to raise their voices, but you yell often?
> 3. Choose One Model Moment: Pick one area this week where you will intentionally model Level 10 behavior, even when it's difficult. For example, staying calm in traffic, showing gratitude in a stressful moment, or sticking with a commitment you'd rather drop.
> 4. Ask for Feedback: Invite someone you trust (your spouse, a student, a colleague) to share what they see in your example. Be open to the truth…it may surprise you.

Role models don't just influence lives; they shape legacies. A Level 10 life isn't just about reaching your own potential, it's about inspiring others to reach theirs.

And the most powerful way to inspire isn't by what you say. It's by how you live.

4

Discipline Over Excuses

Every one of us is either living by discipline or living by excuses. The two can't coexist.

Excuses are easy. They roll off the tongue without effort: *"I don't have time." "I'll start tomorrow." "I'm too tired." "It's not fair."* Excuses feel comforting because they let us off the hook. They soothe us in the moment by shifting blame. But in the long run, excuses steal opportunities, weaken character, and guarantee regret.

Discipline is harder. It requires commitment when you don't feel like it. It demands consistency when nobody is watching. It forces you to confront your weaknesses and push through them. But discipline pays you back in confidence, freedom, and success.

The path to a Level 10 life is paved with discipline. Excuses only lead you in circles.

Restarting Again and Again

When I look back on my martial arts journey, I see both excuses and discipline.

As a teenager, moving back and forth between Indiana and Minnesota was disruptive. Every time I switched schools, I had to restart training, learn new instructors' styles, and rebuild momentum. It was frustrating. And instead of embracing discipline, I leaned on excuses. I told myself it wasn't my fault. I convinced myself that I'd get serious later.

The truth? I had plenty of opportunities to keep training. But I let breakdancing, music, friends, and teenage fun take priority. My purple belt years stretched out far too long, not because of circumstances, but because of my excuses.

Later, when I finally recommitted to training with discipline, I saw progress. Every class, every practice, every repetition added up. In time, I earned my black belt, but it took me nine years instead of the usual three or four.

Nine years, because I chose excuses before I chose discipline.

That experience taught me something I've carried into every part of my life since: excuses delay your destiny, while discipline delivers it.

Discipline Is Freedom

On the surface, discipline feels restrictive. It says "no" to laziness, "no" to quitting, "no" to easy distractions. But in reality, discipline is freedom.

- Discipline in health gives you the freedom to live with energy instead of pain.
- Discipline in finances gives you the freedom to build wealth instead of drowning in debt.
- Discipline in relationships gives you the freedom of trust and respect, instead of the weight of regret and broken promises.
- Discipline in training or learning gives you the freedom of skill, mastery, and confidence.

Excuses promise freedom in the moment but enslave you in the long run. Discipline feels like sacrifice in the moment but frees you in the future.

Excuses in Every Role

- Parents: Excuses often sound like, "*I don't have time to sit down with my kids,*" or "*They'll figure it out on their own.*" But your children need your intentional guidance. Discipline is choosing to be present even when you're tired.
- Teachers and Coaches: Excuses say, "*These kids just don't listen,*" or "*That class can't be helped.*" Discipline says, "*I'll find a new way to reach them. I'll show up tomorrow with the same energy.*"
- Business Owners: Excuses say, "*The economy is bad,*" or "*There's too much competition.*" Discipline says, "*I'll learn. I'll adapt. I'll keep growing.*"
- Students: Excuses say, "*The test was unfair,*" or "*I'm just not good at this.*" Discipline says, "*I'll study harder. I'll train more. I'll keep showing up.*"

The truth is, everyone has excuses. The difference is whether you live by them or push past them.

Discipline Creates Momentum

One of the most powerful aspects of discipline is momentum. At first, discipline feels heavy, like pushing a car uphill. But once you get it moving, discipline begins to carry you.

I saw this with my students. Some of them struggled to even make it to class twice a week at the beginning. But once they built the habit, showing up became automatic. Their discipline created momentum, and momentum carried them toward success. **Momentum is a gift excuses can never give you.**

Discipline Is a Choice

Here's the truth: discipline doesn't care about your feelings. You don't have to feel motivated to be disciplined. In fact, discipline shows its power most when motivation is gone.

- Motivation says, *"I feel like it."*
- Excuses say, *"I don't feel like it."*
- Discipline says, *"I'll do it anyway."*

Every day, you are choosing one of those voices.

Level 10 Takeaways

- Excuses delay your destiny. Every excuse pushes your goals further away.
- Discipline is freedom. It costs in the moment but pays back for life.
- Momentum matters. Small acts of discipline, done consistently, build unstoppable progress.
- You can choose. Excuses feel natural. Discipline must be intentional.

PRACTICAL EXERCISES

1. List Your Excuses: Write down the top three excuses you use most often. Be brutally honest.

2. Flip Them: For each excuse, write the disciplined response. Example: "I don't have time" → "I will schedule 30 minutes."

3. Build Momentum: Pick one small area (health, parenting, study, work) and commit to one disciplined action every day for a week. Track it.

4. No Excuse Zone: Choose one part of your life where you will eliminate excuses entirely. For example: "I will not excuse myself from missing class," or, "I will not excuse myself from treating others respectfully."

Excuses or discipline, you can't live by both.

Excuses give you comfort today but regret tomorrow. Discipline challenges you today but rewards you for life.

The question is not whether you'll face the choice, it's which one you'll choose.

And the truth is, choosing discipline once makes it easier to choose it again. The habit builds on itself until discipline becomes not just what you do, but who you are.

That's when you begin to live at Level 10.

5

Building Something from Nothing

Every dream starts small. Sometimes so small it looks like nothing at all.

That's how my martial arts school began, just an idea, a vision, a hope that I could take what I loved and turn it into something that changed lives. There was no guarantee it would work. There was no safety net waiting if it didn't. It was simply me stepping out into the unknown, trying to build something from nothing.

And I'll be honest, it didn't come easy.

Six Years of Struggle

For the first six years, I struggled more than I succeeded.

I loved teaching. I loved the energy of the students, the challenge of helping kids grow in discipline and confidence, the joy of seeing parents light up when their child achieved something new. But love alone doesn't pay the bills.

The truth was, I didn't know what I was doing when it came to running a business. I thought passion was enough. I thought that if I was good at martial arts and cared deeply about my students, everything else would fall into place.

It didn't.

There were times when I wasn't sure if the school would survive. I made mistake after mistake, financially, organizationally, even personally. I leaned on hope instead of systems. I confused hard work with smart work.

Those six years were a humbling lesson: passion without structure is not enough. Heart without strategy can only carry you so far.

The Turning Point

At some point, I realized that if I didn't change, my school wouldn't survive.

That's when I made one of the most important decisions of my life: I invested in mentorship. I paid thousands of dollars, money I didn't really have, for people to teach me how to run a business. I invested in my education, not just as a martial artist, but as an instructor, a leader, and an entrepreneur.

It wasn't easy to admit that I didn't know what I was doing. But that humility was the turning point.

I traveled across the United States and overseas to China, Korea, and the Netherlands to sharpen my skills and broaden my perspective. Every trip was a reminder that if I wanted to build something lasting, I had to build myself first.

And slowly, things began to change. My school grew stronger. The systems improved. The finances stabilized. What once felt like "barely hanging on" became a thriving program that has now influenced thousands of students and families.

Lessons in Building

Looking back, here are the truths I learned about building something from nothing:
1. Passion is the spark, but it's not the engine. Passion will get you started, but discipline, strategy, and humility keep you going.
2. Mentorship saves years of mistakes. Yes, it costs money. But the cost of ignorance is always higher.
3. Growth requires humility. You can't build something new while clinging to the belief that you already know it all.
4. Invest in yourself first. If you're not growing, what you're building can't grow either.

For Parents

Building something from nothing isn't just about businesses, it's about families, too. Parents are building little humans into strong, capable adults. And just like my first six years in business, parenting rarely comes with a manual. It's messy, unpredictable, and humbling.

But the same principles apply. Don't just lean on love, create structure. Don't just assume your child will "figure it out," invest in mentorship, books, resources, and communities that make you a stronger parent. Don't let pride stop you from asking for help.

Building your child's future is the most important construction project you'll ever take on. Treat it that way.

For Teachers and Coaches

Every classroom and every team starts with nothing. You walk in on the first day, look at a group of faces, and wonder, *"What will this become?"*

The temptation is to think you're just teaching a subject or a skill. But the truth is, you're building character, culture, and confidence. You're shaping people who will go on to shape the world.

That's building something from nothing. And it requires patience, humility, and long-term vision.

For Business Owners

You already know what it feels like to start with nothing. You've faced the blank page, the empty room, the unreturned calls, the quiet seasons.

The question isn't whether you'll struggle, the question is whether you'll persevere. Will you learn what you need to learn? Will you invest in yourself? Will you humble yourself enough to ask for help?

Building something from nothing is possible, but only if you're willing to grow faster than the thing you're building.

For Students

If you're a student, you may feel like you don't have much to work with. Maybe you don't have the talent of others. Maybe you don't have the resources. Maybe you don't feel like you're "ahead."

But here's the truth: every black belt, every teacher, every leader, every champion started exactly where you are, at nothing. What matters isn't what you start with, but whether you commit to the process. The student who shows up consistently, who studies a little each day, who trains even when it's boring, will always outgrow the student who has talent but no discipline.

Level 10 Takeaways

- Building starts with humility. Admit what you don't know, then seek help.
- Ignorance is more expensive than education. Pay the price to learn now, or pay a bigger one later.
- Your greatest investment is yourself. The stronger you are, the stronger what you build will become.
- Persistence outlasts obstacles. Most people give up before they see results. Don't.

> **PRACTICAL EXERCISES**
>
> 1. Name Your Project: Identify one area of your life where you're building something from scratch (a business, a family, a skill, a goal).
> 2. Find the Gap: Write down what you *don't* know that's holding you back. Be specific.
> 3. Seek a Mentor: Find one person, book, or program that can help you close that gap. Invest in it.
> 4. Commit to the Long Game: Write a sentence you can repeat to yourself when the struggle feels too long. For example: *"I am building something worth the fight."*

Building something from nothing is never easy. It will test you, stretch you, and humble you. But it will also grow you into someone stronger than you ever thought possible.

Because at the end of the day, what you're really building isn't just a business, a family, or a dream, it's yourself.

6

Investing in Yourself

If there's one lesson that has transformed my life more than any other, it's this: the best investment you'll ever make is in yourself.

Not in stocks, not in real estate, not in shiny new equipment. In *you*.

Because when you grow, everything you touch grows with you, your family, your students, your business, your influence. If you don't grow, they stagnate with you.

I had to learn this lesson the hard way.

The Cost of Ignorance

In the early years of running my school, I struggled because I simply didn't know what I was doing. I thought hard work and passion would be enough. But no matter how many hours I put in, it felt like I was spinning my wheels.

That's when I realized something painful: ignorance was costing me more than education ever could.

Yes, it cost money to hire mentors. Yes, it cost time to attend seminars and workshops. Yes, it cost humility to admit I didn't know what I thought I knew.

But the price of staying stuck, financial stress, sleepless nights, the constant fear that I might lose my dream, was far higher.

So I began investing in myself.

Paying the Price to Grow

I spent thousands of dollars, money that often felt impossible to spare, on mentors who could teach me how to run a school successfully. I didn't just buy their advice; I bought back years of trial and error.

I traveled across the United States and even overseas, to China, Korea, and the Netherlands, studying martial arts, business, and leadership. Every trip, every seminar, every training was an investment. It wasn't always convenient, but it was always valuable.

I poured money, time, and energy into sharpening myself because I realized that my school would only grow to the level that *I* grew. If I didn't get better, nothing else would either.

And every investment paid dividends, not always immediately, but always eventually.

The Return on Investment

Here's the truth: the return on investing in yourself is exponential.

- When you grow your knowledge, you gain skills that serve you for a lifetime.
- When you grow your discipline, you create habits that multiply success.
- When you grow your character, you build trust that strengthens every relationship.
- When you grow your vision, you inspire others to grow with you.

People often look at the cost of education, mentorship, or training and think, *"That's too expensive."*

But what they fail to calculate is the cost of *not* investing. Ignorance always costs more than learning. Settling for "good enough" always costs more than striving for excellence.

For Parents

Investing in yourself as a parent doesn't mean spoiling yourself with luxuries, it means sharpening yourself so you can lead your children well.

- Read books on parenting and leadership.
- Attend seminars that stretch your perspective.
- Seek out other parents who are a step ahead of you and learn from them.

Your children will grow to the level of the example you set. If you want them to live at Level 10, you must show them what that looks like by investing in your own growth.

For Teachers and Coaches

The best teachers are always students first. If you ever stop learning, your teaching will stagnate.

Invest in your craft. Study new methods. Observe other great instructors. Go to workshops. Read, listen, and practice.

Your students don't just benefit from your knowledge, they benefit from your growth mindset. When they see that you are still learning, they learn to value learning themselves.

For Business Owners

The success of your business will rarely surpass the success of your own leadership.

If you're struggling in your business, ask yourself: *Am I investing in myself as a leader?*

That might mean hiring a coach, joining a mastermind group, or attending an industry conference. It might mean reading more books, listening to podcasts, or simply carving out time to reflect and plan.

Your business can't grow unless you do.

For Students

Investing in yourself doesn't always mean money, it often means time.

- Study when you'd rather scroll.
- Practice when you'd rather play.
- Read when you'd rather watch.

Every minute you invest in your future self will pay you back. And here's the secret: most students won't do it. That means if you do, you'll be years ahead before you even realize it.

Removing the Excuse of Cost

One of the biggest excuses people make is, *"I can't afford to invest in myself."*

But the truth is, you can't afford *not* to.

You don't have to start big. You can start with a $15 book. A free podcast. A daily habit of reflection. The dollar amount doesn't matter, the principle does. When you invest in yourself, you're making a declaration: *I am worth it. My growth matters. My future matters.*

The more you act on that declaration, the more your life will rise to meet it.

Level 10 Takeaways

- Ignorance costs more than education. Pay now to learn, or pay later in regret.
- Your growth is the ceiling. Your family, students, or business will only grow as much as you do.
- Start small, think big. Even small investments compound over time.
- The best investment multiplies. When you grow, everything you touch grows with you.

> **PRACTICAL EXERCISES**
>
> 1. Audit Your Growth: Write down the last five ways you've invested in yourself (books, seminars, coaching, training). If the list is empty, that's a red flag.
> 2. Budget for Growth: Decide on an amount of time and/or money you will invest in yourself each month. Even $50 or five hours can change your trajectory.
> 3. Pick One Mentor: Identify one person, living or through their work, you can learn from this year. Take one step to engage with their material.
> 4. Create a Growth Ritual: Choose one daily or weekly habit (reading, journaling, training, studying) that becomes your anchor for self-investment.

Investing in yourself may feel costly in the moment, but it's the one investment guaranteed to pay back for a lifetime.

And as you continue to grow, you'll discover that the return isn't just personal, it's generational. Your children, your students, your employees, your community… they will all rise to the level of the investment you're willing to make in yourself.

Because when you unleash your own potential, you give everyone around you permission to do the same.

7

The Teacher Within

There's an old saying: *"When the student is ready, the teacher appears."*

What I've learned over the years is that sometimes, the teacher who appears... is *you*.

We often think of teaching as something reserved for professionals, schoolteachers, coaches, instructors. But the truth is, every one of us is a teacher. Parents are teachers. Leaders are teachers. Older siblings are teachers. Even students are teachers, because the moment someone looks up to you, you've stepped into the role of a teacher whether you planned on it or not.

And the most surprising part? Teaching doesn't just shape the student, it transforms the teacher.

How Teaching Became My Calling

When I first started teaching martial arts, I thought it would simply be a way to share what I loved. I didn't realize how much it would demand from me, or how much it would change me.

I discovered quickly that teaching wasn't just about transferring knowledge. It was about patience. It was about communication. It was about learning how to break down something I had practiced a thousand times into steps that made sense to a beginner.

I couldn't just demonstrate a kick, I had to explain it, repeat it, and find three different ways to describe it until the student understood. And in doing that, *my own mastery grew*.

Teaching clarified my thinking. It forced me to slow down, to analyze, to refine. I realized that you don't truly know something until you can teach it.

That realization reshaped my life. Teaching wasn't just something I did, it became my calling.

The Double-Edged Gift of Teaching

Teaching is one of the few things in life that rewards both the giver and the receiver.

- The student grows in knowledge and skill.
- The teacher grows in clarity and mastery.

This is why I encourage my students, especially the younger ones, to turn around and help the person behind them. When a white belt asks a yellow belt for help, and that yellow belt explains something simple, both of them grow. One learns the move, and the other strengthens their own understanding by explaining it.

Teaching unlocks the teacher within all of us.

Parents as Teachers

If you're a parent, you're the most important teacher your child will ever have. Schools can provide education, coaches can develop skills, but you are the one who teaches values, resilience, and character.

- When you model respect, you're teaching.
- When you handle conflict calmly, you're teaching.
- When you follow through on commitments, you're teaching.

- And yes, when you lose your temper or break your promises, you're teaching then too.

Your children are always in your classroom, whether you realize it or not.

Teachers and Coaches

Formal teaching carries its own challenges. You'll face students who resist, who don't want to learn, who push your patience to the limit. But those students are often your best teachers.

The child who struggles forces you to find new ways to communicate. The one who acts out teaches you the importance of consistency. The one who quits reminds you that teaching isn't about controlling outcomes, it's about planting seeds.

Every challenge a student brings is sharpening you as much as it shapes them.

Leaders as Teachers

If you're a business owner, manager, or leader, you're teaching every day. Your employees are learning what's acceptable based on your behavior. Your clients are learning what you value by how you serve them. Your team is learning what you expect by what you tolerate.

Leadership *is* teaching. And the most effective leaders understand that their job isn't just to instruct, it's to inspire, to equip, to guide.

Students as Teachers

You may not think of yourself as a teacher yet, but if you're a student, someone is always watching you. Younger kids in the class are copying how you train, how you treat others, how you handle mistakes.

Even outside of class, your friends learn from how you respond to pressure. Your siblings learn from how you deal with failure. Your peers learn from the example you set, whether it's positive or negative.

When you embrace the fact that you're already a teacher, you begin to take your role more seriously. And that's when growth multiplies.

Teaching Forces Growth

The greatest gift of teaching is that it forces growth.

When I prepare to teach, I have to study harder. When I explain something, I have to simplify it. When I correct a student, I have to examine my own habits.

Teaching stretches you in ways nothing else can. It sharpens your awareness. It multiplies your patience. It deepens your humility.

Because the moment you step into the role of teacher, you're not just responsible for your own success anymore, you're responsible for someone else's. And that weight makes you stronger.

Level 10 Takeaways

- Everyone is a teacher. Parents, leaders, students, we all influence someone.
- Teaching multiplies growth. The student learns, and so does the teacher.
- Challenges sharpen the teacher. Difficult students, employees, or kids are opportunities in disguise.
- Teaching requires humility. You can't teach well if you believe you already know it all.

PRACTICAL EXERCISES

1. Identify Your Classroom: Write down one area of life where you are already teaching others, whether you've realized it or not.
2. Teach to Learn: Pick one concept you know well and explain it to someone else. Notice how it deepens your own understanding.
3. Model the Lesson: Ask yourself, *"Am I living the lesson I want others to learn from me?"* If not, what needs to change?
4. Seek a Student: Find someone behind you in the journey and intentionally teach them one thing this week.

The teacher within you is one of your greatest untapped resources. You don't have to wait for a classroom, a title, or a position. The moment you recognize that someone is watching you, learning from you, and following your example, you realize the teacher was always there.

The only question is, what kind of teacher will you choose to be?

8

Respect, Focus, Discipline

Every strong system, whether it's a family, a classroom, a business, or a martial arts school, rests on a foundation of values. Without values, you drift. Without values, you compromise. Without values, you lose sight of who you are and what you're building.

At my school, three values have guided us since day one: Respect, Focus, and Discipline.

They are more than words on a wall. They are the heartbeat of everything we do.

Respect: The Beginning of Greatness

Respect is where it all begins.

In martial arts, respect is built into everything. We bow when we enter the mat. We bow to our instructors. We bow to each other. Some people think it's just tradition, but it's far more than that.

Respect is about acknowledging the value of others. It's about humility, the recognition that you're not the center of the universe.

I've seen tournaments where schools show incredible skill but terrible attitudes. Students strut with arrogance. Parents argue with judges. Instructors let pride overshadow humility. And I've seen how that ruins the experience, not only for themselves but for everyone around them.

By contrast, our school has a reputation at tournaments for the way our students and parents carry themselves, with humility, kindness, and honor. Judges and coaches have approached me to compliment not just our skill, but our character. That, to me, is worth more than any trophy.

Respect is the foundation of greatness because it grounds you. Without it, success only inflates your ego. With it, success becomes a platform to serve and inspire.

Focus: The Power of Attention

If respect is the foundation, focus is the fuel.

We live in the most distracted generation in history. Phones buzz constantly. Notifications steal our attention. Entertainment is available 24/7. Focus has become a rare commodity.

But focus is the difference between mediocrity and mastery.

When I was stuck at purple belt for years, one of my greatest weaknesses was lack of focus. I trained, but I didn't train with consistency or intentionality. My attention was scattered, part martial arts, part breakdancing, part distractions. And my results reflected it.

When I finally committed to focus, everything changed. Instead of dabbling, I drilled. Instead of drifting, I showed up. Instead of wishing, I worked.

Focus is like a magnifying glass, it takes scattered light and channels it into fire.

- Parents who focus on their kids, not just with their presence, but with their attention, change their children's confidence forever.
- Teachers who focus in the classroom inspire students to believe they matter.
- Leaders who focus their vision give their teams clarity.

- Students who focus in practice progress twice as fast as those who only "show up."

Focus is power. Without it, potential leaks away. With it, ordinary effort becomes extraordinary.

Discipline: The Glue That Holds It Together

Respect sets the foundation. Focus fuels the journey. But discipline is what makes it last.

Discipline is the daily choice to do what needs to be done, especially when you don't feel like it.

It's the parent showing up for their child even after a long day. It's the teacher staying patient with the student who just isn't getting it. It's the business owner making the calls, balancing the books, and facing the hard truth instead of hiding from it. It's the student tying on their belt and stepping onto the mat, even when they'd rather stay home.

Without discipline, respect and focus fade into intentions instead of outcomes. Discipline is the glue that holds the values together.

Living the Three Together

Respect, Focus, and Discipline are powerful on their own, but together they create something unstoppable.
- Respect keeps you humble.
- Focus keeps you effective.
- Discipline keeps you consistent.

I've watched students who embody all three transform not only their martial arts, but their lives. They carry themselves differently at school. They take responsibility at home. They lead in ways their parents never imagined possible.

And I've seen the opposite, students who refuse respect, who scatter their focus, who lack discipline. No matter how much talent they have, they stall out. They may shine for a moment, but they never last.

The same is true for families, classrooms, and businesses. Without respect, focus, and discipline, they crumble. With them, they thrive.

Level 10 Takeaways

- Respect grounds you. Success without respect leads to arrogance.
- Focus multiplies effort. Attention turns average into excellent.
- Discipline sustains growth. Daily choices matter more than bursts of effort.
- Together, they create transformation. Respect, Focus, and Discipline are the triad of a Level 10 life.

PRACTICAL EXERCISES

1. Respect Audit: Ask yourself, *"Do the people closest to me feel valued by how I treat them?"* Write down one way you can show respect more intentionally this week.

2. Focus Check: Identify your biggest distraction. Commit to eliminating it, or limiting it, for one week, and channel that time into something that matters.

3. Discipline Challenge: Choose one habit you know you need to build and commit to doing it for 21 days. No excuses.

4. Teach the Triad: Share these three values, Respect, Focus, Discipline, with someone else, and explain how you're working to live them out. Teaching it will reinforce it.

Respect. Focus. Discipline.
Three simple words. Three powerful values. Three life-changing habits.

If you build your life on them, you'll stand tall no matter what storms come your way. And if you teach them to others, whether as a parent, a teacher, a leader, or a student, you'll create a ripple effect of excellence that lasts long after the moment has passed.

Because a Level 10 life isn't built on chance. It's built on values strong enough to withstand time.

9

The Level 10 Leader

Leadership isn't about titles, positions, or recognition. True leadership is about influence, about helping others become more than they believed they could be.

I've held the title of "Grandmaster," but the title itself doesn't make me a leader. What defines me as a leader is the students I've raised up, the lives I've impacted, and the example I've chosen to live every day.

One of the greatest honors of my life was promoting four of my own students to 5th Dan. In our system, that moment is significant, not just for them, but for me. When you promote a student to the rank of Master, you are recognized as a Grandmaster.

That experience taught me something profound: leadership isn't measured by what you achieve personally. It's measured by what you help others achieve.

The Weight of Leadership

Leadership carries a weight that can't be ignored. When you step into leadership, whether in a family, a classroom, a business, or a community, you are saying, *"I will go first."*

- Parents go first by modeling integrity, humility, and consistency for their children.
- Teachers go first by showing patience, discipline, and persistence in front of their students.

- Business owners go first by setting the standard for work ethic, culture, and service.
- Students go first by showing younger peers what it looks like to commit, persevere, and respect others.

When you lead, people are watching. They are learning from you, whether you intend it or not. That's why leadership is as much a responsibility as it is a privilege.

Leadership Is Service

The greatest leaders aren't the ones demanding recognition, they're the ones quietly serving.

Leadership isn't about power. It's about responsibility. It's about asking, *"How can I make those around me better?"*

When I promoted those students to 5th Dan, I wasn't thinking about my recognition as a Grandmaster. I was thinking about the years of sacrifice those students had made, the nights of training, the weekends at tournaments, the perseverance through injuries and setbacks. My role as a leader wasn't to shine in that moment, but to lift them up into the spotlight they had earned.

That's what real leadership looks like.

The Mirror of Leadership

Here's the hard truth: the people you lead will reflect you.
- If you're inconsistent, they'll be inconsistent.
- If you gossip, they'll gossip.
- If you cut corners, they'll cut corners.

But the opposite is also true:
- If you stay disciplined, they'll rise to discipline.
- If you show humility, they'll mirror humility.
- If you lead with respect, they'll carry respect with them.

The people closest to you are a mirror of your leadership. If you don't like what you see in them, start by looking at yourself.

Leadership Requires Courage

Leadership isn't easy. It requires courage.

Courage to set high standards, even when people resist. Courage to make hard decisions, even when they're unpopular.

Courage to take responsibility, even when failure isn't entirely your fault.

Courage to stand alone, if necessary, to do what's right.

Mediocrity will always try to creep into your team, your family, your classroom, your business. A Level 10 leader has the courage to push it back, to call people higher, to refuse to accept "good enough."

Leadership in Every Role

- Parents: You are your child's first and most important leader. The way you lead at home will set the tone for their entire life.
- Teachers and Coaches: You are shaping far more than skills. You are shaping confidence, character, and resilience. Don't underestimate the influence you hold.
- Business Owners: You set the culture. Your employees will work as hard, or as little, as you do. Your clients will sense your values in how you serve them.
- Students: Even without a title, you're a leader. Younger kids look up to you. Your peers notice how you train, how you behave, how you treat others.

Leadership isn't about position, it's about example.

Level 10 Takeaways

- Leadership is influence. It's not about titles; it's about impact.
- Leadership is service. The best leaders lift others higher.
- Leadership is a mirror. The people you lead will reflect who you are.
- Leadership requires courage. The courage to set standards, take responsibility, and stand for what's right.

> **PRACTICAL EXERCISES**
>
> 1. Leadership Mirror: Identify one area where those you lead are reflecting a weakness in your example. What needs to change in you first?
>
> 2. Lift Someone Up: This week, find one person you influence and intentionally encourage them. Recognize their effort, not just their result.
>
> 3. Set One Standard: Choose one standard you will hold firm in your family, classroom, or business. Communicate it clearly and live it out.
>
> 4. Serve First: Ask yourself daily, *"Who can I serve today?"* Leadership always starts with service.

Leadership at Level 10 isn't about climbing higher, it's about lifting others with you.

Because in the end, the true measure of a leader isn't how far you've gone, it's how far those who followed you have gone because you chose to lead.

10

Overcoming Family Struggles

Every family has its battles. Some are small, arguments over chores, disagreements about curfews. Others are larger, strained relationships, broken trust, deep wounds that leave scars.

For me, family life growing up was often difficult. There were moments of love, but there were also moments of pain. The instability, the arguments, the absence of consistency, it all left a mark. At one point, after an argument with my mother, I ran away from home and spent two weeks living in an empty apartment on my newspaper route. When I returned home, I was sent to live with my father in Minnesota. Moving between homes, states, and schools made me feel like I was always starting over.

Those experiences shaped me deeply, not just as a person, but as a parent, teacher, and leader. They taught me that struggle in the family can either break you or build you, depending on how you choose to respond.

Pain Can Fuel Purpose

It would have been easy to let my childhood struggles turn me bitter. I could have used them as excuses. I could have said, *"This is why I can't succeed."* But instead, I chose to let the pain fuel me.

Every unstable moment taught me the value of creating stability for others. Every harsh word taught me the power of encouragement. Every time I felt overlooked reminded me to see the potential in others.

That's the choice we all face: will family struggles define us, or refine us?

The Parent's Role in Struggle

Parents often wrestle with how much to protect their kids from struggle. The natural instinct is to shield them. But while protection is important, overprotection can rob children of resilience.

Sometimes, the best thing you can do for your child is not to rescue them from every challenge, but to walk with them through it.

- Let them face disappointment.
- Let them wrestle with frustration.
- Let them learn that setbacks aren't the end.

You don't need to make life easy for your kids, you need to make them strong.

As Jim Rohn once said: *"Don't wish it were easier. Wish you were better."*

Teachers and Coaches in Family Struggle

Many teachers and coaches underestimate how much family struggles spill into their classrooms and teams.

I've seen kids walk into martial arts class carrying invisible baggage, anger from a fight at home, sadness from feeling unseen, fear from instability. Their kicks and punches weren't just physical, they were emotional outlets.

That's why teachers and coaches must do more than just teach skills. We must provide stability, encouragement, and a place where respect, focus, and discipline create a safe framework. For some kids, your classroom or team might be the only consistent, stable environment they have.

And that means your influence is greater than you realize.

Business Leaders and Family Struggles

Even in the workplace, family struggles follow people in. An employee dealing with chaos at home will carry that stress into the office. A team member wrestling with family pain will show it in their focus and energy.

Leaders who recognize this reality, and respond with both empathy and standards, create healthier, stronger teams. It's not about lowering expectations; it's about leading with understanding while still calling people higher.

A Level 10 leader acknowledges that family struggles are real, but refuses to let them become permanent excuses.

Students and Family Struggles

If you're a student dealing with family challenges, hear this: your struggle does not define you.

Yes, it hurts. Yes, it feels unfair. Yes, it may make life harder than it seems for others. But it can also make you stronger, wiser, and more resilient than most of your peers will ever be.

Your family's struggles are part of your story, but they don't have to be your identity. You have the power to write a new chapter.

Lessons From the Struggle

Looking back on my own journey, here's what I've learned about overcoming family struggles:

1. Struggles build resilience. Running away, starting over, living with instability, it forced me to adapt, to survive, to toughen up.
2. Struggles create empathy. When I see a student acting out, I don't just see the behavior, I see the possibility of pain behind it.
3. Struggles clarify values. Because of what I lacked growing up, I built my school, and my life, on values like respect, focus, and discipline.
4. Struggles fuel purpose. My childhood taught me that I wanted to create stability, encouragement, and growth for others.

Level 10 Takeaways

- Family struggles can refine you. They don't have to define you.
- Pain can become purpose. Use what hurt you to build what heals others.
- Parents must balance protection and resilience. Don't rescue your kids from every challenge, equip them to handle it.
- Your influence matters. Teachers, leaders, and mentors can provide stability where families fall short.

> **PRACTICAL EXERCISES**
>
> 1. Reframe the Struggle: Write down one family struggle you've faced. Ask yourself, *"How has this refined me instead of defined me?"*
> 2. Choose One Lesson: Identify one positive value you've gained from a painful experience. Example: instability → resilience, harshness → patience.
> 3. Break the Cycle: Write down one pattern you've seen in your family that you refuse to repeat. Replace it with a new pattern of growth.
> 4. Give What You Needed: Think of something you wished you had as a child, encouragement, stability, consistency, and give it intentionally to someone in your life now.

Family struggles are universal. But they don't have to be life sentences.

When you choose to rise above them, you don't just change your own life, you change the legacy of everyone who comes after you.

Because overcoming family struggles is not just about surviving the past. It's about building a future where the cycle of mediocrity ends, and the cycle of strength begins.

11

The Fight for Excellence

Excellence doesn't happen by accident. It doesn't fall into your lap because you got lucky, or because you were born with talent, or because the conditions were just right.
Excellence is a fight.
It's a fight against laziness.
A fight against distraction.
A fight against fear.
A fight against mediocrity.
And if you want to live a Level 10 life, you must be willing to step into that fight every single day.

Excellence Requires Design, Not Chance

One of the most important lessons I've learned as a martial arts instructor is that excellence never just "shows up." You can't hope your way into it. You have to *design* for it.

That's why we structure our training at my school with intentional systems, black belt tests that span years, curriculum that builds layer upon layer, programs like our Shaolin Summer series that stretch students physically, mentally, and even spiritually.

I don't leave a student's growth to chance. I design an environment where excellence is not only possible but expected.

Excellence must be pursued deliberately. If you don't design for it, you will drift into mediocrity.

Excellence Demands More

Excellence is not about doing what's required, it's about doing *more* than what's required.

In martial arts, that might mean throwing one more kick after you're tired, practicing one more round of your form when you'd rather sit down, or stepping onto the mat for sparring even when you're nervous.

In life, it's the same.

- Parents pursuing excellence don't just provide, they model.
- Teachers pursuing excellence don't just instruct, they inspire.
- Business owners pursuing excellence don't just manage, they innovate.
- Students pursuing excellence don't just pass, they master.

Excellence is not about checking the box. It's about raising the bar.

The Enemy of Excellence: Average

The greatest threat to excellence isn't failure, it's average.

Failure at least teaches you something. It forces you to reflect, to improve, to adapt. Average, on the other hand, numbs you. It convinces you that "good enough" is fine. It lulls you into comfort, and comfort kills growth.

When I was stuck at purple belt for five years, it wasn't because I failed, it was because I accepted average. I trained enough to get by, but not enough to excel. I told myself excuses that kept me comfortable, instead of pushing myself toward excellence.

Average is easy. Excellence is rare. But only excellence leads to a Level 10 life.

Excellence Inspires Others

One of the most powerful parts of pursuing excellence is the way it inspires others.

I remember the first time I saw my Master perform a form. His power, precision, and presence captured me. I thought, *"That's what I want to be."*

Years later, when a master told me, *"You're starting to look like your Master,"* it meant more than words could capture. Excellence doesn't just elevate you, it pulls others upward.

When you fight for excellence, you don't just change your own life, you create a ripple effect that impacts everyone watching you.

Excellence in Every Role

- Parents: Excellence is not perfection, it's consistency. It's showing up every day with love, patience, and presence, even when you're tired. It's raising your kids to believe that "good enough" is not their destiny.
- Teachers and Coaches: Excellence means refusing to let students settle for less than their best. It's holding high standards with compassion and persistence.
- Business Leaders: Excellence means creating systems, culture, and habits that push your team forward. It's not about doing more work, it's about raising the quality of the work.
- Students: Excellence means working harder than your peers. It's studying when others are distracted, practicing when others quit, and committing to mastery, not mediocrity.

Excellence looks different in every role, but it's always about raising the standard.

Excellence Is a Daily Choice

The fight for excellence doesn't happen once. It happens every morning when you wake up.

- Will you choose excellence in how you treat others?
- Will you choose excellence in how you manage your time?
- Will you choose excellence in how you pursue your goals?

Excellence isn't a finish line you cross, it's a decision you make, day after day, until it becomes who you are.

Level 10 Takeaways

- Excellence requires design. You can't drift into it, you must structure for it.
- Excellence demands more. It's not about meeting requirements, but exceeding them.
- Average is the enemy. Comfort kills growth; excellence demands discomfort.
- Excellence inspires others. When you raise your standard, others rise with you.

> **PRACTICAL EXERCISES**
>
> 1. Audit Your Standards: Write down one area of life where you've been settling for "good enough." What would excellence look like there?
>
> 2. Add One More: In your training, work, or relationships, choose one place this week to do "one more", one more rep, one more act of kindness, one more hour of focus.
>
> 3. Design for Growth: Build a system or habit that forces excellence, whether it's scheduling daily practice, setting weekly family check-ins, or creating a standard in your business.
>
> 4. Inspire Someone: Share your pursuit of excellence with someone else. Invite them to raise their standard with you.

Excellence is never accidental. It is always intentional. It is always fought for.

The fight isn't easy. It never will be. But it is worth it. Because when you live at Level 10, you don't just achieve more, you become more.

And in becoming more, you give others permission to do the same.

11

Living at Level 10

Living at Level 10 isn't about perfection. It's not about never failing, never stumbling, or never struggling. It's about how you choose to live in spite of those struggles. It's about refusing mediocrity, raising your standards, and committing to be better today than you were yesterday.

It's about living with intention.

A Level 10 life doesn't happen by accident, it happens by design, by values, by habits, and by choices.

The Everyday Choice

Every morning when you wake up, you face a choice:
- Will I settle for mediocrity today, or will I fight for excellence?
- Will I live by excuses, or will I live by discipline?
- Will I complain about my circumstances, or will I rise above them?

The truth is, you don't build a Level 10 life in giant leaps. You build it in small, consistent decisions.
- The decision to respect others even when they don't respect you.
- The decision to focus when distractions call your name.
- The decision to stay disciplined when quitting feels easier.

- The decision to stand back up after you've been knocked down.

Level 10 is not a destination. It's a lifestyle.

What Level 10 Living Looks Like

So what does it look like to live at Level 10?

- As a Parent: It looks like modeling the values you want your children to live. It's teaching them resilience by letting them struggle, and strength by showing them consistency.
- As a Teacher or Coach: It looks like refusing to let students settle for average. It's holding high standards and giving the patience, encouragement, and discipline needed to help them meet them.
- As a Business Owner or Leader: It looks like serving your people, raising the culture, and being the example you want your team to follow.
- As a Student: It looks like showing up consistently, working harder than your peers, and refusing to let failure define you.

Level 10 living looks different in every role, but it always has the same heartbeat: raise the standard.

The Power of Values

Respect, Focus, and Discipline.

These three values have shaped my school, my teaching, and my life. But they're not just martial arts values, they're life values.

- Respect keeps you humble.
- Focus makes you effective.
- Discipline makes you consistent.

When you live these values daily, you don't just create a Level 10 life for yourself, you create a culture that lifts everyone around you.

Your Legacy of Leadership

One of the most profound truths I've learned is that leadership isn't measured by what you achieve, it's measured by what you inspire others to achieve.

When I promoted my students to 5th Dan, earning recognition as a Grandmaster, the moment wasn't about me. It was about them. Their achievement became my achievement, because leadership is about lifting others higher.

That's true for all of us. Parents, teachers, leaders, students, we all have people looking up to us. The legacy you leave isn't in your titles or trophies. It's in the people you've raised, encouraged, and equipped to live at their own Level 10.

No Excuses, No Mediocrity

At the end of the day, mediocrity is always waiting. It will whisper excuses in your ear, tempt you with comfort, and try to convince you that "average" is good enough.

But excellence is waiting, too. And it's your choice which one you'll live by.

No excuses. No mediocrity.

Just the relentless pursuit of the best version of yourself.

Level 10 Takeaways

- Level 10 is a lifestyle. It's built in small daily choices, not one-time achievements.
- Your roles matter. Parent, teacher, leader, student, you can live Level 10 in every arena.
- Values are anchors. Respect, Focus, and Discipline keep you grounded and growing.
- Leadership is legacy. What you inspire in others will outlast you.
- Mediocrity is a choice. So is excellence.

> **PRACTICAL EXERCISES**
>
> 1. Your Level 10 Vision: Write down what a Level 10 life would look like in your role, parent, teacher, leader, or student. Be specific.
> 2. One Daily Standard: Choose one area of life where you will raise your standard this week. Commit to it with discipline.
> 3. Find Your Why: Write down the reason you want to live at Level 10. Keep it somewhere you'll see it every day.
> 4. Lead Someone Higher: Identify one person you influence and challenge them to raise their standard. Lead by example.

The Challenge

Living at Level 10 isn't easy. It never will be. But the rewards are worth every fight, every sacrifice, every moment of discipline.

Because when you choose Level 10, you don't just transform your own life, you create a ripple that impacts your children, your students, your team, and even generations to come.

So here's my challenge to you: Don't settle. Don't drift. Don't let mediocrity rob you of the life you were meant to live.

Unleash your Level 10 life. And in doing so, give others permission to unleash theirs.

Epilogue: Your Next Level

By now, you've seen what a Level 10 life looks like. You've read stories of failure, persistence, and victory. You've seen how mediocrity creeps in quietly and how excellence must be fought for daily. You've learned that respect, focus, and discipline are more than words, they're the foundation of transformation.

But here's the truth: reading this book changes nothing on its own. What matters is what you do next.

A Level 10 life is never about perfection, it's about progress. It's about raising your standard today, and then raising it again tomorrow. It's about committing to one more rep, one more act of kindness, one more moment of discipline when mediocrity is whispering in your ear.

The beauty of this journey is that there's always another level. No matter how much you've achieved, no matter how far you've come, there's always room to grow. There's always a next step, a higher standard, a deeper lesson.

That's what makes life exciting.

So here is my final challenge to you:

- As a parent: Lead your children by example. Show them that mediocrity isn't their destiny.

- As a teacher or coach: Demand excellence with patience and persistence. Shape more than skills, shape lives.

- As a business leader: Serve first. Create culture. Build something that outlasts you.

- As a student of life: Never stop learning. Never stop growing. Never stop fighting for your best self.

The world doesn't get better by chance. It gets better because people like you decide to live better, lead better, and expect better.

So don't wait for the perfect moment. Don't wait until it's easier, or until you feel ready. Start now.

Raise your standard. Fight for excellence. Unleash your Level 10 life.

And when you do, you won't just transform your own future, you'll light the path for others to find their next level, too.

www.ingramcontent.com/pod-product-compliance
Lightning Source LLC
Chambersburg PA
CBHW031558040426
42452CB00006B/338